ADVANCE PRAISE FOR
TIME'S A WASTIN'

Alana has artfully captured the heart of where so many women are as they reclaim their happiness and redesign their life. If you are ready for more fun, meaning and adventure in your life—*Time's A Wastin'* is for you.

—Jane Deuber

Business Strategist for Visionary Entrepreneurs

I loved *"Time's A Wastin'"*. Alana is obviously a woman with strength and compassion. Her stories show how loving, clever, and wise she is. Alana touches on universal issues that all of us can relate to and offers such beautiful insights so we can see things from a different perspective. Her stories are engaging and funny. I loved reading them and loved the thoughtfulness they provoked in me. I will be sharing this book with many of my loved ones!

—*Moneeka Sawyer*

Purpose Coach

Inventor of BlissRetreat.Net

Alana never ceases to amaze me. From the very first day I met her she's been down to earth, authentically genuine, and full of enthusiasm for life. Now she's converted this enthusiasm and zeal into a contribution to others—the empty nesters of our world. Her grounded wisdom and matter of fact prose gently nudges the reader (empty nester or otherwise) to take a refreshing look at life after kids.

—*Ken Larson*

High Performance Executive Coach,

President, Champion Performance Systems Inc.

Time's A Wastin'

Life Lessons Realized As An Empty Nester

Alana L. Newton

DEDICATION

To MY HUSBAND, Smokey, who constantly shows me undying love and support so I can follow my dream. You are my best friend. I love you.

To my parents, biological and otherwise, thank you for sharing your life lessons with me. I know your love for me comes from the depths of your soul.

To my best girlfriends, Diane and Myrna, who always tell me the truth and love me unconditionally.

To my children, Christopher and Shannon, who I know are proud of me, even though sometimes they think I am a bit off the wall.

To the children and grandchildren in our blended family—thank you for accepting me for who I am.

I believe that all the people whose paths have crossed mine have contributed in some form or fashion. There are no accidents, and I know that I have learned many of my life lessons from you.

I have had many teachers, so this goes to all of you in my life—past, present, and future. I am grateful for your love and your teachings.

CONTENTS

PREFACE

THIS BOOK IS A LABOR OF LOVE, full of memories and stories. My intention is to share inspiration and hope with those who relate to my experiences.

By sharing some of my significant life events, and looking at the intuitive signs that tell us there is something else better, it's my hope that you will begin to believe there is something greater than yourself and you will develop your own inner sense of knowing. Though I guess I have always had a sense of knowing there was something greater than myself, for a long time I negated so many of the messages I was getting. We can call it God, Mother Earth, Spirit, the Universe, or whatever you feel comfortable with. I use all of them at different points in my life.

If you are floundering in uncertainty, my greatest wish is that you will learn how to get yourself out of it. If you are wondering what is next for you in any given circumstance, I promise you can have your own answers by paying attention to what is going on from the inside.. Sometimes it is as easy as just asking.

My job as a coach is to ask the questions that will unveil those answers within. The intention is to allow you to think big, outside of your own paradigm, to allow your greatness to come through.

Much love,

Alana

Time's A Wastin'

Alana Newton

1

IN THE NEIGHBORHOOD

Our beliefs can move us forward in life
—or they can hold us back.

—Oprah Winfrey

AT THE AGE OF 10, I was the only kid in the neighborhood with her own phone. A pink one, no less. I will never forget it. It was a rotary dial phone and it was on a telephone desk right outside my bedroom. I remember thinking that this was important and I had a very responsible job. Being the oldest child, I took the responsibility entrusted to me seriously. I had to do the right thing.

The reason I had it wasn't because I was some lucky girl, or that we were well off, or that I talked on the phone with friends. I had it because there were times I needed to call the police for help when my stepfather got violent with my mom. I don't remember how often I had to call, but there were times I was glad it was there.

My mom never really talked about these incidents. She was the bravest woman I have known. She protected my two brothers and me, and never flinched when there was trouble. She stood tall and never backed down. She was tough, because she had to be.

Mom would step up and get another job when it was needed, and she held us together through thick and thin. Money was tight back in the 60s, and she did what she had to do. I remember at one point she held three jobs.

I learned by her example to dig deep, to do whatever it takes. Complaining was for sissies. I was also reminded continuously to not talk back, to keep quiet. What I had to say didn't really matter, so it was best to keep quiet. Children should be seen and not heard … remember hearing that? I was the feisty one, always had lots to say, and spoke out quite regularly. My brother was the quiet one, and my baby brother was too young to know any different.

When I was four or five, I was encouraged to sing and perform and was always told how smart and cute I was. There was so much love around me. I was confident, did well in school, and had lots of friends. I can remember singing "He's Got the Whole World in His Hands" at a local theater where they held talent shows. Myself and three other girls skipped first grade, so we were considered the "smart ones" in the school.

My mom, who was a single mom until I was nine, usually worked a night shift. When I was five, one day I was at my friend's place for a birthday party, and my friend's brother was cutting the grass in the yard. While I was running, I slipped and fell in front of the push lawnmower and lost my ring finger on my right hand! Someone ran and woke up my mom. She and I went to the hospital in a utility truck. I don't remember very much except all the attention I got upon coming home from the hospital. The doctors managed to do the surgery required to re-attach my finger, and re-attach the tendons. Other than a bit of disfigurement, my finger works marvelously, and oddly enough is the only finger on my hand that doesn't have arthritis!

Because my mom worked the night shift, my grandma and aunt looked after us most of the time. Grandma taught me how to iron, crochet, and embroider. Back then, even the pillow cases were ironed. My aunt is only eight years older than I am, and she took me skating and to the movies. I have very fond memories of those times. Life was full and good, and other than the freak lawn-mower incident, I didn't have a care in the world.

But then, when I was nine years old, my circum-stances and my whole life changed. I remem-ber coming home one day to find out that my mom had gotten married, and we were moving! So many things changed so quickly. It felt like my whole world came crumbling down. I didn't want to leave my grandma's house. It seemed like we were moving so far away.

Looking back, I know it was also tough for my mom. She was always trying to keep the peace, run a smooth household, minimize conflict between everyone, and at the same time work on her marriage. Our new stepfather seemed to constantly grumble and complain at my mother about us kids and what we were doing.

This was back in the early 60s, and the norm was to not talk about what went on in your home. We certainly never spoke about the abuse and violence. It was nobody else's business, and "we don't air our dirty laundry in front of others." Today, I recognize that we had family secrets.

I can probably count on one hand the times I saw my mother drink, but my stepfather was another story. As I look back and think about the friends who also had parents that drank a lot, those parents usually fought, and there was physical abuse in their families too. We just never talked about it. It was like it was a normal occurrence. I can even remember thinking, as a young girl, that this was what marriage and having a husband was all about! Who knew it could be different?

Underneath all of this were the subliminal messages and stories I repeated to myself over the years. To my detriment, I held on to some of these stories for over 50 years! I could have been freer then, even freer than I am today, if only I had known better.

You probably know some of these stories and messages—those things we think about when we put ourselves down:

▶ What I say doesn't matter

▶ Listen and don't speak

▶ You'll never be able to do X. You're not smart enough. You're too short, too fat, too …

▶ Stop dreaming

Despite all that, I remember yearning to be someone important. My goals were to work in an oil company, and marry a rich man. That was my statement in my graduation yearbook! Those dreams seemed so far out of my reach back then. Yet I could feel there was another much deeper level inside me.

Looking back, I know now that all I ever really wanted was to get back to being that little girl who felt so brave, so loved, and supported by the important people in her life. I wanted my family to be proud of me.

Isn't that what we all want on some level?

How did things get pushed so far out of proportion, lost, and turned into these negative stories for all these years?

My Lesson

The "stories" I listened to for all those years held me back from pursuing my dreams. Sometimes these negative messages to myself about myself were not really the way things were, but somehow I believed them, and held on to them.

Alana Newton

2

CHOICES

*When someone shows you who they
are the first time, believe them.*

—Maya Angelou

THE FIRST GUY THAT EVER REALLY PAID ANY
ATTENTION TO ME WAS IN 12TH GRADE. I was
16. We became an item, and I fell in love for
the first time. The ideas I had developed about

marriage and husbands became true, because he, like my stepfather, drank a lot and got physically and mentally abusive with me. I didn't realize how wrong it all was, because I didn't have any other frame of reference. For about a year, I was hoping he was going to change. I kept thinking, *If only I could make him happier, we have a chance.* I used to think it was *my* fault that he drank and carried on, because that was what he told me. Deep down, I was hoping he would ask me to marry him, because I really wanted to get out of my house. In my mind, the situation was getting worse at home, and it had to be better with him, because I was going to work hard to please him. I ignored all the signs that said otherwise.

One of the signs was a twinge I would get in my belly, an uneasy feeling, and the thought, *This isn't a good thing.* It was like I had a little man on my shoulder telling me whether to do something or not do it. I call this gut instinct. Now I know to listen to it, but back then, I just ignored the senses and signs. More often than not, if I would have only listened, I might not have suffered as much as I did.

Something deep inside me told me there had to be more than this, and I broke off the relationship—not knowing I was pregnant at the time. I was so naïve, and my head was in the sand. I kept hoping it would all go away. I was a little chubby so I managed to stave off any queries until I was about six months pregnant. Frankly, I was in complete denial—and so afraid. I kept hoping it wasn't so. If it was, then what would I do? How could I explain this one?

In 1970, it wasn't cool to be unwed and pregnant, and a lot of stigma surrounded girls who were. I wasn't "one of those girls," though. I just made a bad choice in my boyfriend. I left our family home and stayed with family friends to have the baby, to save my brothers from embarrassment. Again, more family secrets!

Today I understand how difficult it must have been for my mom to have her only daughter in such a predicament. She lived with guilt and shame and was constantly hearing about it from her husband as if it was her fault. It wasn't her fault, it was mine to bear and mine to resolve. I just didn't know what to do. By the time I stopped being in denial about the pregnancy, I learned that the baby's father was in jail. I was only 17, just out of high school, with no real means to support myself, let alone a baby. I tossed around my options a lot and wrestled with my decisions. I realized there weren't any real options for me. I kept second guessing myself, being logical, then illogical, and going through the "what ifs" over and over, until I made the decision to give up the child for adoption at birth.

I used that gut instinct more than I was really conscious of at the time. This was a huge decision, and wasn't to be decided upon lightly.

My hope and dream was that this child would be adopted by loving parents who could afford to give him a good home and a life full of love, attention, and a good education. A dream I have held on to all these years.

My Lesson

Trust my instinct. If my "spidey sense" is aroused, pay attention. Let go of the need to please everyone in spite of what I am sensing.

Alana Newton

3

FIGHT OR FLIGHT

I trust so much in the power of the heart and the soul; I know that the answer to what we need to do next is in our own hearts. All we have to do is listen, then take that one step further and trust what we hear. We will be taught what we need to learn.

—Melody Beattie

ABOUT A YEAR LATER, the next guy came into my life. At the start, we had a lot of fun. On the surface, things looked like they were going to go somewhere. We had mutual friends, and it seemed like all of our friends were getting married around that time. When we had been going together about six months, he finally asked me to marry him, and I jumped at the chance. Our engagement lasted about another six months, and during that time, all the warning signs were there. During our engagement I experienced abuse, infidelity, and instability—and yet, once again, I didn't listen to my inner self.

Part of me tried to tell me numerous times to get out of the relationship, but I ignored it and turned a blind eye. I just wanted so desperately to feel loved and wanted, and I thought that if I was a good wife, things would turn for the better.

We actually separated at one point, after a year of marriage, but after about four months we got back together. We were in a terrible car accident which catapulted us into getting together again.

It wasn't all bad, don't get me wrong. We had some really good times, and we had two wonderful children together. The children became my life and focus. They were my whole world, and everything was centered around them. I thoroughly enjoyed nurturing and teaching them. They were the main reason I stayed so long in the marriage—because I didn't want to be a single mom like my mom had been. Everything I did was with the intent of maintaining stability in their lives.

We also had some really rough times. In hindsight, I see that a lot of history from my own childhood repeated itself in my children's lives.

I firmly believe that unless we know we have a choice and make a decision to behave differently and break the cycle, history can and does repeat itself.

I can't remember a time where we weren't trying to survive or overcome an obstacle. We had big dreams; however, that's all they were. We never had plans to work towards those dreams. We had no goals, only "what ifs" and "somedays."

I was a good wife. I always supported whatever my husband wanted to do. We tried geographical cures four separate times to see if that would make a difference in the marriage. He worked, I stayed home. He stayed home, I worked. Whatever we did, it didn't work.

I am not certain if it was stubbornness or being too naïve to listen to those "little messages" that we get when our inner self wants to get our attention, but it took me a long time to make the decision I needed to make. There were many times where he would take off and go out on a drinking binge. He was unfaithful far too many times to count. The last straw was when he started being abusive to our son, and he pointed a shotgun at my chin while he pinned me against the fireplace.

Our marriage was in its tenth year when I had finally had enough.I knew it was time to go. I fled and took my children, who were six and two years old at the time. I believe pure survival instinct kicked in and I did what I had to do. All I wanted for us was to be safe and feel loved.

When it is necessary to make quick, tough decisions, it doesn't take rocket science to figure out what needs to be done. There was no nudge or twinge here. It was a hard, solid choice.

So there I was, landing back in my hometown with no place to live. All I had was what I could take with me in the back of a pickup truck, and my two precious children. Thank goodness my brother and his friend came to rescue us. I am grateful for my brother having let us stay with him for a bit until I could figure out what to do. I was hoping I would get back to our home and get the rest of our things at a later date, but it never happened. A few months later, a neighbor called, telling me our house was burning to the ground. The children and I were literally starting out all over again.

I had no money, and was challenged with going to the local welfare office to get help. I specifically remember standing in line in the freezing cold two days before Christmas, waiting for a food hamper for the children and me. I finally got to the front of the line, only to learn that my social worker had not submitted our names. I borrowed 25 cents to use a pay phone on the corner and called my social worker in tears, with no idea what I was going to do for food over Christmas.

I vowed right there and then that this would never happen to us again. I found us a decent place to live and went back to school. Then I dropped out so that I could take control of my life, get a job, and provide for my children. In hindsight, had I stayed in school, my life would have been much different. I was learning to be a computer programmer before computers were even popular. I see where that career could have taken me. I guess I just had more lessons to learn.

Take control of my life is what I did. I got a job in a bar that paid reasonable tips in addition to an hourly wage so that I could support my family. I had a good caregiver for the children, and life was ticking along just fine.

My Lesson

Messages and signs show up when you need them. I had to take drastic action, which first took becoming aware and trusting in myself.

4

PRIORITIES

One can find women who have never had
one love affair, but it is rare indeed to
find any who have had only one.

—François de La Rochefoucauld

HERE WE GO AGAIN! I met another man, and
he seemed different. He had a steady job, was a
hard worker, and also fun-loving. He fell in love

with my kids, and they really liked him. I wasn't looking to get into a relationship, given what I had just come out of. But he was very persistent and convincing.

Soon enough I got those "nudges" again, telling me that something wasn't quite right. Once again, I didn't listen to them. After all, I knew how to handle anything … right? The first sign was that we had met in a bar where I worked.

How is it that our feelings for a person can completely overrule the "signs and senses" and our better judgement? *Besides*, I thought, *it can't happen again. He's different, he works, and the kids like him.*

We eventually moved in together, bought a house, and life was moving along. I got a good steady job in an office, Monday to Friday, which replaced the income I was making at the bar. No more working nights and missing out on my kids' lives.

After about a year and a half, once again I found myself in a position where I was trying to keep the peace for the sake of the relationship and the children. I didn't like where I was at. I was compromising, making excuses, always trying to people please, and gave up so much of myself in the process. Meanwhile, he was constantly grumbling at me—just like my stepdad did to my mom.

Our relationship was deteriorating rapidly, and the stress of all of this was beginning to take its toll on me. I was starting to have health issues. Abusive behavior was on the rise, and it was a horrible environment to be living in. There was little joy, happiness, or love in our home at that time. We were just going through the motions.

I was in my mid thirties, and besides relationship issues, I was dealing with a great deal of stress with my son, and he and his sister needed all of my attention. I didn't have the energy or desire to keep this relationship going.

Finally, after seven years of being together, we agreed that he would leave. It was hard on us both, because I really did love him.

Going from two incomes to one added to the stress, and pressure was mounting about how the children and I were going to survive.

Are you starting to see a pattern here? Do you see patterns that have shown up in your own life experiences?

Meanwhile, amidst all this personal drama, I was working my way up to a promotion in my job.

I eventually became one of the first female managers in an all-male Canadian/Japanese family business. In addition to working, I took courses two nights a week and did my homework on Saturday nights after the kids had gone to sleep. I was determined that our lives were going to be different. I was getting good vibes from all of this. All I ever wanted for us was to be safe, and feel loved and supported.

 **My Lesson**

I had to concentrate on what was really important, and put some of my own needs aside for a while. My children were the most important thing in the world to me. This was the one thing I knew for sure.

Alana Newton

5

ALL IT TOOK
WAS ONE BOOK

*We must assume every event has significance
and contains a message that pertains to our
questions ... this especially applies to what
we call bad things ... the challenge is to
find the silver lining in every event,
no matter how negative.*

—James Redfield, in *The Celestine Prophecy*

IN THE LATE 1980S, I was introduced to the book *The Celestine Prophecy*. Once I started reading it, I couldn't put it down! Have you ever had that happen? I was mesmerized by what I was reading.

It talked about all the things I had thought about over the years, such as coincidences, "nudges," and inclinations … and I was so relieved that I wasn't crazy! Other people felt these things too! That felt really good.

I would put this book right up there as the sole (or soul) reason I began my own spiritual journey of exploration.

It showed up at a time when my son was having a great deal of difficulty. I genuinely thought I might lose my mind. I was a single mom, trying to go to school, with a son who was having difficulty with his behavior in school. I was blessed to have him placed in some very focused counseling. However, after he had been there for over two weeks, the counselors were seeing no progress. My son refused to do the work necessary for the program he was in.

His counselor asked me if I believed in God. I guess I did ... I think. I really only prayed to God when I was in distress. I taught my children to say bedtime prayers and say grace, probably only because that was what I was taught to do. I had no basis for religion or spirituality. Never questioned it or discounted it. I was neutral.

I was in such a dark place, and so desperate for my son to find his peace, that I was ready to follow whatever the counselor told me. He suggested that I pray to God and ask him to let this young man know that if he makes the right choices, he will see the rewards. I did this for three days, and on the fourth day my son agreed to do the work necessary. He was one thousand miles away from me, so I know I certainly didn't have the power to make that happen. I believe today that a miracle occurred, because I believed and asked.

Eventually, the children and I were able to get into some family counseling to deal with our issues, and this is when I truly believe I was led to begin my own journey of self-discovery and healing.

We worked hard as a family, and I think it was tougher on me than on the children. Believe me when I say that children thrive on boundaries, even though they like to push them and challenge them. My life was in such chaos that I would say one thing and then renege on what became an empty threat. With the help of counseling, we learned to set boundaries and determine the marks of authority between myself—the parent, and them—the children.

What shows up in your life that you have a sense of "knowing" about? How do you listen to it? What steps do you take?

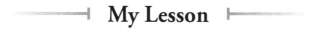 **My Lesson**

Never, ever give up. Answers will come. Have faith and trust in this knowing.

Pay attention to the messages that show up when you are in need of guidance.

Alana Newton

— 6 —

ONE DAY AT A TIME

When you get good at living your present moments one day at a time, you'll see yourself changing right before your own surprised eyes.

—Anita Moorjani

MY CHILDREN AND I WERE SO BLESSED to have received the necessary help to be able to heal as a family and repair the harm that had been caused by so much dysfunction.

I began my own transformation and recovery during this time as well. I struggled with being "addicted to the alcoholic," and it was in those rooms where I learned so much about my own insecurities and how my old "stories" held me back from happiness and joy.

I began to understand my own behavior, and caught a glimpse of a spiritual way of living that wasn't chained down by some religion. I was getting excited! I was feeling free and finding my own inner peace.

It was in those rooms that I learned about really caring for myself. There was peace in our home, and through that peace came strength. Strength to trust my own inner guidance, to find my peace and serenity.

I quickly saw how with just a little faith and work, I would witness miracles in my life and in my friends' lives.

I met my best friend in this program, over 20 years ago. Today, we can talk on the phone without having chatted for weeks, and pick up right where we left off.

Once we had stabilized, things were going along just fine. I became somewhat complacent, figuring "I got this," rather than maintaining my daily practice of gratitude and humility. I used to journal, focus on first things first, stay in touch with my spirituality. Then I slacked off on those habits. I felt certain that I could handle anything that came my way. And it did come, believe me!

I started seeing the man I had lived with five years previous, and it was obvious that there was still some love there. I had a different outlook, because I had done a lot of personal work. He, however, hadn't changed one bit! I knew this instinctively, but I figured I could handle it. He wanted to reconcile, so we made it legal this time and got married.

I clearly remember having those "gut sensations" around this huge decision I had just made, that were in direct conflict with all I had been working toward in my own life. I ignored them, and very soon in the marriage I found myself going back to that old toxic and unhealthy behavior. My 15-year-old daughter even said to me one day, "Mom, what happened to you? You were so strong and spiritual, and now you aren't, because you are giving up who you are again." She was right.

What had happened to my spiritual life, my gratitude and strength?

After many attempts to make this marriage work, it was obvious that I couldn't stay any longer. I still loved him, but I was not willing to be treated with disrespect and bullied. I knew that I was responsible for my own peace and happiness, and that he wasn't. If I was to keep my sanity, I needed to go. So I did.

My Lesson

I can only change myself, and nobody else. It's not my job to fix others.

Alana Newton

7

CONVERSATIONS

Life begins at the end of your comfort zone.

—Neale Donald Walsch

I HAD GIVEN UP SO MUCH OF WHO I WAS WHEN I HAD RECONNECTED WITH THIS MAN. I knew I needed to get back into alignment with my highest self.

I truly believe we are on this earth for one reason—to live a life of purpose. If we don't yet know what that purpose is, we must continue to follow the various options put in our path until it feels absolutely right and true for us. Until that time, we will continue to learn, grow, and in many cases continue to suffer, if that is the way we choose to do it.

There were a lot of steps I had to take to get back on my journey. Suffice it to say, I learned a great deal about myself. Again.

The first thing I did was surround myself with people who thought the way I did—people who were positive and had a lot of optimism. I had been living in so much negativity that it was important for me to live on the other side of that.

My spiritual well-being had also suffered, so I connected to a couple of communities that could support me spiritually. I learned how to meditate. I listened to audio recordings of people I admired and looked up to, such as Dr. Wayne Dyer, Deepak Chopra, Marianne Williamson, and Gary Zukav. I began to explore using some Native American traditions such as sweet grass and sage. I made sure my home was a reflection of who I was, and that it was safe and loving.

By this time, my children were moving out and getting on with their lives. There were some days, sitting alone, that I wondered if the only thing I did right was raise my children. I was all alone ... but I was excited! I was on a journey, not knowing the destination.

The next book that came to my attention was *Conversations with God* by Neale Donald Walsch.

I knew exactly what he was talking about, because it was how I had been feeling for years! I couldn't put the book down! I was in awe and wanted more. I talked about it to friends, and to whoever would listen. I was building a community around this book and it was so gratifying to be able to hold deep, meaningful conversations with like-minded people.

One of the profound statements I read in this book, was, "Your soul doesn't care what you do for a living … and when your life is over, neither will you. Your soul cares only about what you are being while you are doing whatever you are doing." I took this to mean that I must live for my highest good, so that I can serve others and help them do the same. What is really important, and what I need you to know, is that it is okay to start over again … and again … and again …

 # My Lesson

No matter what, you will be okay.

Alana Newton

8

THROUGH
THE TUNNEL

*It's fine to celebrate success, but it is more
important to heed the lessons of failure.*

—Bill Gates

PRIOR TO LEAVING THE MARRIAGE, I had changed
jobs and taken on a huge responsibility with
over 20 staff. It was also a self-help organization

and it aligned with some of my own principles. My life got very busy. I made sure of that!

In many of the positions I have had throughout my career, I found myself having to reorganize, fix, restructure, or rebuild. I can honestly say that I left each organization in a better state than when I arrived. I pride myself on that! All of this came at a cost though … it required commitment, hard work, dedication, and a little bit of insanity. That attitude of "do whatever it takes." (Thanks, Mom!)

I was working 50-60 hours a week and on call 24/7. My organization supervised former federal and provincial prisoners who were out in the community on parole, and it was a very high stress job.

I was officially a single "empty nester." I remember thinking those words, and thinking "So, what the hell does that mean?"

What it meant for me was that I was alone with nobody to go home to or cook for. It was just me, myself, and I. Sometimes, on Friday nights, I had popcorn for supper! I took on a part-time home based business, mostly for the social aspect, in addition to my job. I filled my calendar to where I didn't have any time for me. Truth is, I wasn't aware I needed to take time for myself.

I wanted so badly to do a good job and gain the respect of a few important people in my life. I negated my subconscious thoughts about getting back to my spirituality and listening to my inner voice. I slid back into the numb avoidance of what was going on around me. I was still connected with my community, but I was only showing up, not fully present.

I pushed through each day. I did a lot of shopping for material things, because it always made me feel better—for a short time. I worked all the time, staying just sufficiently out of touch with reality to not admit how bad my reality was. I was lonely, scared of being alone, and really didn't know who I was. I even tried my hand at an affair with a married man … which in the end made me even lonelier. Basically, I realized that I had filled all my time with stuff that wasn't meaningful or valuable. I was lost. I didn't know what I was passionate about. I didn't know my purpose. I thought of leaving my job, but didn't know where to go or what to do.

After I had been on the job about five years, our organization had a critical incident, involving a murder that one of our clients committed, and it was horrific for the staff, the board, and me (the CEO) to go through what we did. To this day, when I think about it, all the old awful memories and feelings come back. The incident had a huge impact on me. I was numb from reading all of the details of the transcripts, and overwhelmed by the depositions I had to make. It was very lonely at the top. It wasn't appropriate to confide in the staff. I had a board of directors who were volunteers, and it wasn't their job to get me through this. I was the CEO; I couldn't show any weakness, I had to do what was necessary. So I did what most people in that position would do—dealt with it and got on with things.

That was about when I started to experience some minor health issues. I found myself back and forth at the doctor's, and after having had a reaction to some medication, it was suggested I have an ultrasound. I remember lying there while the girl was doing the test. I had an inclination that something wasn't right. I got that twinge and roll in my belly. I told my girlfriend about it as soon as I got out.

My family doctor called me two days later to tell me that they had found a tumor on my left kidney, and further tests would have to be conducted to see what the next steps should be. That was in October. I had renal cell cancer. I had surgery to remove a third of my left kidney in March of the following year.

Waiting and not knowing whether I was going to live or die for those five months was agonizing. I was full of fear! We didn't know for sure how bad it was until the surgery. I began thinking about all the regrets I had. Things I hadn't done. Places I hadn't seen. My kids not married yet, grandchildren I would never meet.

What I knew for sure was that if I were to get through this, my life was going to change … for the better! And that "No matter what, I am going to be okay."

Well, I did get through it! And with no chemo or radiation at that. It was 12 years ago, and I am still going strong.

The key thing I learned through all this was that it is so easy to let things slide back to where they were and get out of control. I was so overcome with stress, loneliness, and negativity, that they overshadowed all the good I had been creating.

My Lesson

Was my lesson!

Alana Newton

9

WHO WAS I?

I have learnt that success is to be measured not so much by the position that one has reached in life as by the obstacles which he has overcome while trying to succeed.

—Booker T. Washington

DURING THOSE MONTHS OF WAITING FOR MEDICAL TEST RESULTS, I had been working with coach Ken Larson. We focused mainly on support for my CEO role, and together we worked on team building, organizational structure, and succession planning. When all this came down the pipe, we then had to focus on an exit strategy for when I was going to be off work.

This relationship was so valuable to me. During the entire time, he was my biggest fan, my rock. He had my back, and kept my spirits high when I couldn't for myself. I will never forget waking up in the hospital and seeing him and his daughter standing at the end of my bed with the biggest bouquet of flowers. He said, "You did it! It's done. It's time to move on with your life!" I have so much love and gratitude for him—beyond words.

I was at home for three months after the surgery, and this afforded me the opportunity to really look at my life and how I wanted to live it.

One day I was sitting in my chair, pondering where I had come from and what was next. Tears starting welling up and soon I was crying. I didn't even know what I was crying about except that I felt so lost, so alone, and didn't know who I had become. I think it was a sense of loss, along with fear of what could have been.

As I look back, I feel I was realizing that part of my whole being was missing. I was lacking joy, peace, faith, and passion. How did I let myself get so out of touch? Not long before, I had been so grounded, grateful, peaceful, and happy. Now I was 49 years old, alone, and with no goals or dreams.

Time to get on with my life? I started writing down things I wanted to do—like travel, places I wanted to see ... and then I wrote the word *Career.* I knew I had to give up my part-time business, because I couldn't carry the crates any longer. What was I going to do? I was going back to my CEO job with a plan.

I had received such value, support, and encouragement from my coach, so I decided to look into becoming a coach myself. At 49 years old, I was going to University—for the first time ever—to become a coach.

I remember how on my application, one of the fears I expressed was that I was worried about whether I was smart enough to be going to University. There's one of those old "stories" again, telling myself that I was *not good enough.* I finished the course with the highest marks possible! Ha! I even surprised myself.

 **My Lesson**

When the student is ready, the teacher will appear. I had to hit bottom to realize how important my life on this earth really is, and that I had a lot yet to do!

Alana Newton

10

DO WHAT MAKES
YOUR HEART SING

Your time is limited, so don't waste it living someone else's life. Don't be trapped by dogma—which is living with the results of other people's thinking. Don't let the noise of others' opinions drown out your own inner voice. And most important, have the courage to follow your heart and intuition.

—Steve Jobs

I became a coach when coaching wasn't cool yet. I had no idea how I was going to make a career of this. All I knew was that through coaching I could help people, like my coach helped me. I did a lot of coaching for free, initially.

I came alive when I was coaching, and I eventually left the stressful organization I had been working with for seven years—this time for the right reason. I wanted to work in alignment with my principles and purpose and the values that mattered most to me. I began having dreams and goals again, focusing on what was important in my life.

My "big rocks" included my own spirituality, my children, my health, and close friends.

This was a time in my life where I started to follow my intuition around what I was aligning with. I took mini-workshops on self-development, courses on personal values, and got another coach to work with. Retreats are probably my most favorite thing to do, even now. This was when I was able to get out of myself and get connected to an environment that is uplifting, focused, and full of growth. I have met some amazing people who I remain in touch with today.

I am telling you all this to highlight how life is a journey, a process. There wasn't one single thing that gave me this new outlook on life. It is a series of events—both tragedies and joyous moments—that get us to where we want to be.

I sold my condo and moved to a completely unfamiliar neighborhood looking for newness, change, and possibility. I had very few visitors, but I was beginning to be at peace. I stayed there a year, and then found another little condo back in my former area of town that I renovated and settled back in to familiar surroundings. At one point I actually contemplated selling everything and moving to the Dominican Republic. I had been thinking about it for some time. I just never had the courage. Besides, what the heck would I do when I got there?

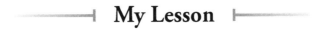 **My Lesson**

It's never too late to wake up and follow your dreams.

11

CONSTANT AFFIRMATION

Sharpening the saw is about constantly renewing ourselves in the four basic areas of life: physical, social/emotional, mental, and spiritual. It's the habit that increases our capacity to live all other habits of effectiveness.

—Stephen R. Covey

A LARGE CORPORATION IN OUR CITY, which practiced the principles of *The Seven Habits of Highly Effective People (Stephen R. Covey)*, chose a few executive directors to be trained as facilitators who could teach these principles. The main goal was to have trained people who could deliver the program to their own teams and companies. I was one of the executive directors who participated, and it was such a gift—life changing and exhilarating.

In addition to the various workshops and trainings, I found the greatest learning in the books I read during that time. They were another way for me to personally grow. I love books whose messages resonate in alignment with who I am. I can highlight them, write in them, and use them over and over.

Some of my favorites are:

▶ The Monk Who Sold His Ferrari
—Robin Sharma

▶ Conversations with God (all of them)
—Neale Donald Walsch

▶ The Four Agreements—Don Miguel
Ruiz

▶ The Celestine Prophecy—James Redfield

▶ The Tenth Insight—James Redfield

▶ A Return to Love—Marianne Williamson

▶ Codependent No More—Melodie Beatty

▶ The Seven Spiritual Laws of Success
—Deepak Chopra

▶ Manifest Your Destiny—Dr. Wayne W. Dyer

▶ The Power of Intention—Dr. Wayne W. Dyer

▶ The Seat of the Soul—Gary Zukav

▶ Men Are from Mars, Women Are from Venus—John Gray

How do you show up for yourself? What do you do for yourself in order to care for your own needs, growth, and learning? How do you go about developing new techniques? Do you practice hobbies? Do you do things to bond with the girlfriends? If you are married, what do you and your husband do together, just for yourselves?

My Lesson

Nobody, no course or book, could do the work for me. I had to want it and do what was necessary to make positive changes in my life.

Alana Newton

12

BLIND DATES

It's a sad day when you find out that it's not accident or time or fortune, but just yourself that kept things from you.

—Lillian Hellman

MY LIFE WAS FULL, and I was healthy and grounded. I was an executive director in the charitable sector for a number of organizations over the span of ten years.

One of the roles I had, and that I thoroughly enjoyed, was contracting in a program that supplied executive directors to organizations that were in transition. I really loved what I was doing.

Organizations undergoing transition in leader-ship, especially in the charitable sector, can be so vulnerable. My role was to work with the Board of Directors of such organizations, to provide guidance and leadership and to coach both management and staff. Common themes in this role were that the staff wanted to feel safe in their jobs and the board needed to know that the organization was running smoothly. For me, it was important to show up fully present and share my experience with both parties.

Somewhere in all this, I had family members telling me that they knew this guy I had to meet. "Life is too short to be alone." "At least go to dinner with him."

Frankly, I wasn't interested. I was settling into liking my life as it was. If it isn't broken, why fix it?

One day, I was watching a football game and got asked to participate in a contest during the third quarter. I agreed, and went down to the assigned area out on the field. I appeared on the jumbo screen at exactly the same time that this guy was up in the stands with his brother-in-law and they were discussing him meeting me. He asked the brother-in-law what I looked like, and he looked up on the screen and said, "There she is!"

The rest is history. I won a large gift certificate for pizza, so the family got together after the game and he came too. It took him about another two weeks to call me, and we went out for dinner.

Neither of us had been out on a "real date" for many years, so once dinner was over, things got awkward. He asked if I wanted to see where he worked, and I was in fact interested, because he was a manager of a large manufacturing plant. So, off we went to check out the plant—in our best clothes and me in heels.

At one point we had to walk around a big piece of equipment in a pit, and he put out his hand to help me around. I knew right there, right then, that this was going to go somewhere.

I had "spidey senses" going off all over, in the best possible way. He was kind yet strong. I felt safe and completely at ease. We had a lot in common and liked a lot of the same things. Having met the way we did, we certainly knew we both liked football!

Our courtship lasted over two years, and then we decided to give living together a chance. I was able to keep up my own personal development along with our relationship, and this was really important to me.

Not long after moving in together, I noticed that I was becoming slightly irritable and feeling like something was missing. I was sliding again, thinking I had to be "super girl" and do, do, do—everything for everyone, except myself. Funny thing is, not once did he ask me to be like that. In fact, he had commented numerous times how he liked that I could take care of myself and knew what I wanted. The stressing out was all my own doing! I realized that I needed to rein in my tendency of pleasing everyone except myself.

Two years later, we married—in our back yard, with all our friends and family. Between the two of us, we have six adult children and five grandchildren.

We have had our ups and downs. When I feel out of sorts, I know it is *my* responsibility to honor myself and ask for what I need. My joy is not fully dependent on him, and I can't expect him to fulfill all my needs. My spiritual practice and my daily personal practices are what keep me grounded. And he supports this wholeheartedly.

A couple of years before meeting my husband, I actually sat down and wrote out what I wanted in a relationship, where I wanted to live, and what kind of life I wanted.

I found that page just a couple of years ago. I saw that I wrote my husband's "job description" to a T. The things that sometimes irk me about our relationship or about my life are things that I forgot to put into that description. Ha! Silly me. You see, I believe the Universe gives us all we ask for. If we don't have something, it's because we didn't ask.

Today, my husband is my best friend. We finish each other's thoughts and sentences, and he is my biggest fan. I am so grateful for all he does for our family. He has gone out on a limb to support me, financially and emotionally, throughout my journey.

Some of the goals that his partnership has helped me achieve include developing my full coaching practice, becoming a speaker and radio show host, and last but not least writing this book. I am so blessed!

Do you see the theme here?

My Lesson

It is our own responsibility to follow our dream, to take care of our own well-being.

Alana Newton

13

MAKING IT WORK

I wish that I did the things that I really believe in, because when I do, my life goes much smoother.

—Cher

SO, LET'S DELVE DEEP INTO THIS MARRIAGE THING. How many of you are married, and have been lonely in your marriage?

I am now a married empty nester, and you know what? It still takes work, and being committed to what is true for me, to live my best life. Some of the issues from before still remain.

I hear similar things all the time from my clients: "We don't do anything together any more." "He falls asleep on the couch every night." "He drinks too much." "The sizzle is gone." "We don't have anything in common."

I get you! I have been through all this, many times. I have felt lonely even when my husband is sitting right across the table from me. I had a huge epiphany about this. Really! I did!

About three years ago, I was sitting there and wasn't sure what was going on with me. I felt lonely, restless, unloved, and insecure. I wasn't having any fun or "playing." Sometimes it felt like my craft room was calling out to me, "Help! Let's play!"

I was slipping again, falling back into people-pleasing mode, worrying so much about everyone else around me that I was last on the list—once again.

I knew I was irritable, not smiling very much, and sometimes difficult to be around. I wasn't working full time, but I seemed to be busy all the time. I had no joy. My closest friends lived too far away to just pick up and go for coffee. I was really missing girlfriend time.

I am so grateful that when I am dealing with something, my husband takes a step back and lets me figure it out. I know he would love nothing more than to get in there and do whatever I want, to make me happy. As they say, "Happy wife, happy life."

But, here's the news flash … IT'S NOT HIS JOB TO MAKE ME HAPPY!

It is each of our job to figure out what makes us tick, to understand what makes us happy, and learn how to find our own joy. Once we have that figured out, we need to communicate it to our partner. Now, and this is important … you don't just figure it out and then tell him what *he* needs to do to make you happy. *We* must take responsibility for our own actions and follow through on them.

What is missing in your life that you wish to have "someday?"

What are you passionate about? If money or time were no object, what would fill that hole in your soul?

And then, I ask, how do you communicate your needs?

Here is what I did: I did some soul searching about what was missing in my life, what I needed in order to feel fulfilled and happy. I signed up for lots of personal development courses. I got a coach.

I still had that dream, that began many years earlier, to become a fulltime coach and help people the way I was helped by my coach. I signed up for a couple of courses to discover how I could help the most people at one time.

I quickly discovered that use of the world wide web seemed to be the way of the future for coaches. I have been following this path now for a couple of years. I am so grateful to Max Simon and Jeffery van Dyk for "myth busting" my old stories. Sometimes I want to quit, because I still allow some of those old "stories" to raise their ugly heads from time to time. As one mentor would say: they are only stories!

But after I have spent time with my clients and witnessed their transformation, those doubts and fears are gone. I am so humbled and honored to coach individuals on their own journey to freedom.

I live each day fully, with intention and gratitude. You can too.

What would it take for you to do your own soul searching? It can be done with a coach like me, or on your own. However you do it, you must do it, for your own sake.

Trust me—your children, your friends, and your partner will thank you for it. You will be happier, feel fulfilled, and have balance and joy in your life.

My Lesson

The journey doesn't have be lonely. Engage with people who will support you.

Alana Newton

14

MY VISION

My Vision for All Women in the World

▶ Women will feel complete and whole

▶ Women will contribute on a much larger scale in this world

▶ There will be less health issues for them

- ▶ They will be respected as great leaders in the world

- ▶ They will be compensated and compared equally – there will be no difference, gender-wise

- ▶ Women will set a new paradigm for their children

- ▶ Men will feel relieved to know that women are responsible for their own happiness

15

TIPS & TRICKS

If you don't know what your passion is,
realize that one reason for your
existence on earth is to find it.

—Oprah Winfrey

IN THIS CHAPTER, I aim to recap some of the techniques I use to check in with my intuition or gut instinct, as well as the daily activities I practice.

Yes or No?

If we are going to show up authentically and stand in our own power, we have to start listening to our inner voice, our inner guidance, and learn to recognize the physical signs we get. I learned a technique to find out how our body can speak to us, and it is so simple.

Here it is:

Stand tall, feet shoulder width apart or slightly closer. Close your eyes, and take a deep breath. Ask your body to show you a "Yes." Keep your eyes closed, and pay attention to what happens. Does your body sway slightly? Side to side, or front to back? Do you get a "nudge" in your belly? The sign can be ever so slight, but it will be there. Pay attention. Now, open your eyes.

Same technique again: Stand tall, feet shoulder width apart or slightly closer. Close your eyes, and take a deep breath. Now, ask your body to show you a "No." What happens? What does your body feel or do?

Write these signs down for future reference.

Personally, I double checked my answers by asking myself some straightforward questions that I knew for certain were "Yes" and "No" answers. Keep on practicing this technique until you know for sure that you can trust your body to give you answers.

_____

_____

_____

Do you have a Dream Board? If not, why not? I won't go into details about how to make one—if you don't know, you can Google it and find out.

_____

_____

_____

What about journaling? It's worth doing, even if it is just for 5-10 minutes each day or writing down 5 things you are grateful for that day.

_____

_____

_____

Do you practice meditation, and what type? If you don't, try it—even if you just sit still for 15 minutes a day and focus fully on your breathing.

_____

_____

_____

Do you have a coach? Have you ever had a coaching session?

Check out what I could offer you at www.alananewton.com

To receive your FREE copy of my ebook, *Reclaiming Your Time*, please go to http://alananewton.com/programs-coaching/ reclaiming-your-time/

Alana Newton

WHAT OTHERS ARE SAYING

DURING THE PROGRAM, I realized that I was actually quite lonely, but too busy to think about it. Sure, I had some family and friends, but it seems like all I ever do is work and do things for others. I am so glad I had a chance to see this for myself. Things are changing! I am actually spending time doing things I love.—Jane G.

Just had the most AMAZING hour with the awesome Alana Newton.—P. Turko

You have a way of connecting with people ... making them feel valued, respected, and heard.—BC Bren

Absolutely, I would recommend Alana as a Business/Life Coach. She has helped me over the past couple of years to walk through needed change. Like many others, sometimes I have been stuck. Sometimes I have known what I needed to do, but have lacked the will power to make change. Sometimes I have lacked clarity as to the steps needed to implement change. Alana has helped me with change—change for the better. As a result, I have experienced more balance and a sense of personal well-being. Thank you, Alana.—L. Gait

Having a coaching session with Alana is like a breath of fresh air. She has the ability to get to the heart of the matter and ask the tough questions, without it feeling invasive. Her insight and honesty have allowed me to look clearly at my situation and see more of the choices I had available to me. I would highly recommend Alana Newton as a coach for anyone who is not clear on their life path or vision.—Kamala Murphey, MA ThM

Alana Newton

IN CLOSING

*He is a success who has lived well, laughed often
and loved much; who has gained the respect of
intelligent men and the love of children; who
has filled his niche and accomplished his task;
who leaves the world better than he found it,
whether by an improved poppy, a perfect poem,
or a rescued soul; who has never lacked appre-
ciation of earth's beauty or failed to express it;
who has always looked for the best in others
and given the best he had.*

—Bessie Anderson Stanley

Alana Newton

ABOUT THE AUTHOR

ALANA NEWTON HAS BEEN IN BUSINESS FOR OVER 40 YEARS, working in both the corporate and non-profit realms, with roles from social worker to media professional to salesperson to executive. After a successful 12-year run in the corporate world, she made the decision to become a CEO in the non-profit sector, in which she remained for over 10 years. Alana has been a board member of nonprofits for over 30 years. Overlapping with both, she has been an entrepreneur for 35 years, running an effective direct sales and network marketing business.

12 years ago, Alana had the "perfect storm" of personal crises that caused her to examine and drastically change her life. At the age of 49, she went back to school and earned a Certificate in Executive Coaching and is a member of the International Coach Federation at the ACC level.

Alana is a spirited coach who knows firsthand what happens when your world is turned upside down because you haven't taken the time to focus on what is really important.

Today, her passion is helping Empty Nester Women—entrepreneurs and executives who are in the overwhelmed and confused state she was in—to move to a life that is as happy and fulfilling as hers is now. To move from a place of busy-ness to a new place of more passion and purpose, and more business. She can help you design a life built around your highest values and deepest desires.

Alana's passion and purpose is seeing women achieve their goals and succeed. She gets excited about personal development, and loves playing a part in helping others achieve the development and growth they desire.

Made in the USA
Charleston, SC
30 December 2014